Find Your Personal Avatar

Heinz Krug

Copyright © Heinz Krug

First edition: December 2021
Publisher: Heinz Krug
Author email contact: heinz@gehirnsoftware.com
Website: avataram.org

Disclaimer

Contents of the book
Author, editor and publisher do not assume any liability for the topicality, correctness, completeness or quality of the information provided. Liability claims against the author or the publisher, which refer to damages of material or immaterial nature caused by use or disuse of the information or the use of incorrect and incomplete information are excluded, unless the author is not intentional or grossly negligent fault.

Health
The purpose of this book is to provide our readers with information on the topics discussed. This book is not intended to be used to diagnose or treat medical conditions. For diagnosis or treatment of medical problems, seek the advice of their physician. Editor, author, or publisher are not responsible for any health or allergy needs requiring medical supervision, nor are they liable for any damages or adverse effects of any treatments, activities, applications, or remedies for persons reading this book. References are for information only and not an endorsement of any websites or other sources.

Copyright and trademark law
The author endeavours to observe the copyrights of the images, graphics, sound documents, video sequences and texts used in all publications, to use images, graphics, sound documents, video sequences and texts created by himself or to use licence-free graphics, sound documents, video sequences and texts.
All brands and trademarks mentioned within the book and, if applicable, protected by third parties, are subject without restriction to the provisions of the respectively valid trademark law and the ownership rights of the respective registered owners. The mere mention of a trademark does not imply that it is not protected by the rights of third parties!
The copyright for published objects created by the author himself remains solely with the author of the book. Any duplication or use of objects such as diagrams, sounds or texts in other electronic or printed publications is not permitted without the author's agreement.

Legal validity of this disclaimer
If sections or individual terms of this statement are not legal or correct, the content or validity of the other parts remain uninfluenced by this fact.

ISBN 978-0-9955961-6-0

avataram.org

10 9 8 7 6 5 4 3 2 1

For the Rose of the Himalaya

The following meditation is available to sing along with:

avataram.org

Meditation

कर्पूरगौरं करुणावतारं
संसारसारम् भुजगेन्द्रहारम् ।
सदावसन्तं हृदयारविन्दे
भवं भवानीसहितं नमामि ॥

karpūragauraṁ karuṇāvatāraṁ
sansārasāram bhujagendrahāram |
sadāvasantaṁ hṛdayāravinde
bhavaṁ bhavānīsahitaṁ namāmi ||

Glistening white like camphor,
The embodiment of compassion,
The essence of the world,
With the king of snakes as garland,
You always dwell in the lotus of my heart,
To the divine, male and female united,
I bow my head.

0. Introduction

Table of Contents

0. INTRODUCTION 6
1. THE TERM AVATAR 9
2. THE UNIVERSE COMPUTER 11
3. THE FIELD OF ALL KNOWLEDGE 15
4. MAGIC OR TECHNOLOGY? 18
5. THE KNOWLEDGE OF THE OMNISCIENT 20
6. THE FUNCTION OF AN AVATAR 23
7. HOW MANY AVATARS ARE THERE? 26
8. THE PERSONAL AVATAR 29
9. HOW DO I FIND MY AVATAR? 32
10. AN ETERNAL RELATIONSHIP 34
11. AT EYE LEVEL 36
12. WHERE DOES MY AVATAR LIVE? 38
13. NEUTRALIZE INTERFERENCE 40
14. ACHIEVE EVERYTHING 42
15. THE POWER OF THE ALMIGHTY 44
16. DIVINE MAGIC 47

Foreword

Dear Reader! The meditation at the beginning on page 5 is probably the most sung verse in India. With great devotion, hundreds of millions of Indians open themselves every day to the Infinite, the Divine. This opening to the infinite divine consciousness within ourselves is the subject of this book.

When I write a book, I always draw inspiration from the divine source. At the beginning of this book came this very verse: 'Karpura gauram ...' I already knew it from my initiation ceremony into mantra meditation and memorized it after several years of regular meditation during my meditation teacher training in 1976. It is the moment of complete surrender of the meditation teacher to the Divine Principle, combined with the invitation to take a seat in his heart and guide him in the right transmission of meditation.

When I now looked at the verse again more closely, the content of the book was clear. The chapters resulted from the words of the verse. For some years now, I have been enthusiastically helping people to reestablish contact with their divine original source. From there, where all knowledge is available in great bliss, it is a joy to bring pure knowledge into one's life. Problems almost solve themselves and this never-ending source of inspiration and joy opens up in daily life.

This process I have called intuition. The knowledge thus gained I called intuitive knowledge. But it was clear to me from the beginning that this is much more than intuition. It is a higher level of consciousness where the divine principle becomes an important part of our own lives. In my book "Brain Software" I refer to this consciousness as the Brain Software version 6. Each higher state of consciousness is simply an improved version of the Brain Software and can therefore be easily and effortlessly installed.

While the ease and speed of the installation process can be simply described as "loading improved Brain Software", it cannot be easily described how grand it is to experience Brain Software version 6. At this stage in the evolution of man, in addition to the brain, the heart is enlivened and the harmony between the heart and brain increases.

Thus, one aim of this book is to awaken and strengthen the enthusiasm for living from the divine original source. Another aim is to show that it does not require long practice to have success. It requires nothing more than a resolve to open yourself to the one Source now and always, and to enjoy life to the fullest from now on. This book is meant to inspire you, dear reader, to take this step, to remove fears and blockages along the way, and to give you the knowledge and confidence that it is a doable and rewarding path.

Living in connection with the Divine Original Source within all of us will bring infinite benefits to the whole Earth. The great misunderstandings in the cognition of truth will disappear. The unsolved mysteries of physics will be solved. One of these is vacuum energy, which can give us access to the power of the Almighty if we dare to tread new paths of cognition.

At the very end I will give an outlook on our future world, a world that is going to have divine magic. We are able to change the world, to make planet Earth a positive example of a fantastic evolution of consciousness. Our home can even become a shining, living example for other worlds. Once we have found our personal Avatar, we can do our part and begin to transform our world into Heaven on Earth.

Heinz Krug, December 2021

1. The Term Avatar

Avatar is a word from the Sanskrit language. It is the original language of humanity. Almost all languages known today are derived from Sanskrit. In the original Sanskrit, one says 'Avatāra'. The letter 'ā' is pronounced long, the 'a' at the end is almost breathed. So we write it as Avatar.

What is an Avatar? It is a descent, a going down, an incarnation. Who or what descends? The Divine descends to Earth and appears in a perceptible way.

On Earth there have been many Avatars, many embodiments of the one divine principle. Among the best known in modern times are Buddha, Jesus, Krishna, Rama, Kuan Yin and the great prophets.

Depending on education and own experiences, people imagine these Avatars very differently. Each person has his or her own image, so to speak, of the Avatar worshipped. This is an important insight.

But it is not only one's own image that makes the Avatar appear as personal. The descent of the Avatar becomes complete for a human only when the Avatar has arrived at him personally. This involves his own character of his Avatar, which can be accepted by the human being. That is exactly what the personal Avatar is.

The infinite Divine is infinitely playful and diverse and so are the personal Avatars. In infinite variety, Infinity presents itself ever new and ever interesting. Where does it present itself? In our perception of the limited, finite world. The infinite plays in the finite. It plays in every plant, every animal, in a beautiful landscape, a force of nature, the oceans and rivers, mountains and hills, the laws of nature, in suns, planets, - moons, galaxies, in the starry sky, and finally, in a perfect way, in our personal Avatar.

Through our personal Avatar, Infinity comes to eye level with us and in this way enables us to have a personal communication. This communication is part of the divine play. With this we can connect to the divine source of all knowledge and receive inspiration, knowledge, solutions to problems, creative ideas without end. How can this happen? I will explain this in the further chapters. There exists a simple way to achieve it quickly and to experience it again and again every day.

For some years now, the term Avatar has also been used in a slightly different way. In computer games, it refers to the game characters with which a player moves in a simulated world. The players then see their Avatars, which move around on screens, but which also lead a life of their own within the simulation of the game world. They can accumulate characteristics and change over the course of a game, depending on what experiences they have already had, what challenges they have faced. Such properties are, for example, energy level, health, wealth, special treasures, weapons, etc.

A game Avatar thus allows its player to immerse himself in the simulated game world and to feel comfortable there. The Avatar is thus actually a bridge between a player and his virtual game world simulation. The word bridge describes the function better than the often used term computer interface. A game Avatar is therefore a communication bridge to the game world that goes beyond the familiar input and output options such as keyboard, mouse, screen, game controller, etc. It brings a human component into the game with which a player can identify more easily.

Thus, the Game Avatar is actually a small replica of the original principle of a real Avatar. Both are communication aids. In one case in communicating with a complex game computer, in the other case in communicating with the infinitely complex infinity of the Divine.

The Avatar as a manifestation of the Divine makes communication with Infinity possible, meaningful and desirable. Only an Avatar enables us to draw from the Infinite Source and to benefit from it again and again. The Avatar brings the abstract Divine Principle to a human level, to eye level. This enables us to communicate with the Divine and allow it into our lives.

2. The Universe Computer

To better understand the Avatar, we must first better understand what the world is. In our opening verse, the word 'sansāra' refers to the world. What is the world in which we live?

To answer this question, I would like to look at the latest findings in physics. For about a century, all physicists have agreed that it is best to view our world from the perspective of quantum physics.

What are quanta? They are the smallest building blocks of nature. Max Planck discovered a special quantum phenomenon in 1900 and Albert Einstein described quanta as a fundamental level of the laws of nature for the first time in 1905, his miraculous year. Until the 1920s, many other physicists developed the so-called quantum mechanics.

Today, quantum physics has come much further. In many areas there is a highly precise correspondence between theory and practice. This means that certain measurable quantities agree very precisely with the theoretical predictions of quantum physics.

On the other hand, there are still many unsolved mysteries of quantum physics. I could write a whole book about that. But what I am particularly interested in now, in order to understand the world better, is the concept of information.

What is information? It is an ordering principle. Through information, order is spread. Information contains within itself an ordering force. The formulas for information and order are almost the same. Don't be afraid. I am not going to write down any physical formulas in this book. Order in physics is the opposite of entropy, which could also be called disorder. Wherever more information is added, entropy decreases and order increases.

Now theoretical physicists in their research for deeper knowledge made a very special discovery a few years ago. Physicists always want to describe the behaviour of elementary particles as simply as possible, but correctly. It turned out that a certain property of a group of elementary particles can be described most simply with a computer code. That is, in this case, the simplest physical formula was a computer code, or more precisely, an error correction code.

What does that mean? It means that quantum physics cannot be the final level of reality. To understand the world properly, we must go beyond quantum physics. To understand what holds the world together inside, we need to understand the information that holds quantum physics together.

More and more influential physicists now agree that the physics of the future will be a physics of information. The study of information is just now becoming an important branch of physics.

So what holds the world together at its core? It is an information network. This network controls the behaviour of all particles and fields at the quantum level. Now it can be shown from computer science that every information network must also be a computer, provided it is large enough and can perform some basic functions. These include the ability to store information at certain points and to pass it on to other points, and also to loop information back to itself.

With these properties, the information network of physics is also a computer. I would like to call it the universe computer. The universe computer is the biggest computer there is. It is at least as big as the universe in which we live.

At the same time, it is also the smallest computer. Its smallest dimensions correspond to the smallest distances that still make physical sense. The physical quantity for this is called the Planck length, in honor of its discoverer Max Planck. It is 1.6×10^{-35} meters.[1] That's 0.000 000 000

---

[1] The ^ character is the superscript. The number after it indicates how many places the decimal point is moved to the left or right. The minus sign before the 35 means moved to the left.

2. The Universe Computer

000 000 000 000 000 000 000 000 016 meters. This is the finest resolution that exists in the quantum space of our universe.

At the same time, the universe computer is also the fastest computer there is. It operates at the speed of light and this results in a clock speed of 10^{44} hertz between the smallest distances. [2] That is 100,000,000,000,000,000,000,000,000,000,000,000,000,000,000 clock cycles per second. Modern office computers today have a maximum clock speed of about 10 gigahertz, or 10,000,000,000 clock cycles per second. The universe computer is ten thousand million million million million million times faster.

At the same time, the universe computer also has the highest memory density, which results from its smallest spatial dimensions. It is so dense that every elementary particle is controlled by it and in the information space of every elementary particle its entire history since the beginning of the universe can be recorded. The storage density of the universe computer can be calculated from the Planck length and it is about 10^{99} bits in every cubic centimeter of space.

If you add up all the technical memories of all the computers on Earth, all the disk drives, all the memory sticks, all the DVDs, etc., and then multiply this number by itself again, you would get about 10^{99} bits. This is how much memory the universe computer has available in every cubic centimeter of space

The universe computer is actually what makes up space itself. The Sanskrit name for space is 'Akāsha'. What is sometimes called the Akashic Chronicle is just one of the functions of the universe computer. It is the function that records everything that has ever happened in our universe. This record is exact. It includes all fields and every elementary particle. In the volume of each particle of matter, there is enough

---

[2] Without the minus sign, the decimal point is moved to the right. ^44 means to move 44 places to the right. So 44 zeros are added to the right of 1.

memory to record the trajectories of that particle since the beginning of the universe. [3]

Another function of the universe computer is to control every smallest particle at every place and at every time. Even if we can only statistically estimate by quantum measurements how a multitude of particles behave, there is actually an exact control of each individual particle by the universe computer. With this control, the universe computer brings order into the apparent quantum chaos. We experience nature as ordered. It follows natural laws. These only come into being through the work of the universe computer. Without the universe computer, an orderly world could never emerge from the apparent quantum chaos.

Another function of the universe computer is to pass on information. It is not limited by the speed of light. Information flows freely in the network of the universe computer. What is nowadays awkwardly described with the so-called quantum entanglement is actually an inherent property of space. Information can flow infinitely fast.[4]

How do we get this information? We only need to gain access from our brain to the universe computer. As soon as we gain access to the universe computer, the entire information store of the universe is at our disposal.

From which level can we sensibly access all this information? It is, of course, the top hierarchical level of the universe computer. From there, any information can be accessed.

---

[3] Most physicists will still disagree with me on this point because they are convinced that elementary particles have no individual properties. But they cannot prove this conviction exactly and sometime they will realize their misunderstanding.

[4] The understanding of what space is, still has to be developed a little further in order to understand this. We still have to find a concept of space that connects quantum space with the space of gravity.

3. The Field of all Knowledge

What is the gist of the world? What is its essence? This question is expressed in our opening verse by the term 'sansārasāram'. To penetrate into the core of being of the world, we have to know it. Knowledge leads us to the essential core. Therefore, we now consider the field of all knowledge.

Vedic science is a way to gain reliable knowledge. Patanjali's Yoga Sutras are an important aspect of Vedic knowledge. In them are recorded all the methods and exercises to develop consciousness. They are something like an instruction manual or a manual for the brain.

The Yoga Sutras distinguish several levels of knowledge. The first level is called Pramana. This is correct knowledge. It is gained by perception, logical reasoning and by recognized experts or teachers. This correct knowledge is always limited and therefore should still be replaced by something better. Each person can have only a limited amount of experiences, read books, listen to lectures. Knowledge gained in this way is always limited. It is roughly equivalent to what we call information. Information still has the flaw that it is not properly interconnected.

The next level of knowledge in the Yoga Sutras is the Jnana. This is a knowledge that is interconnected. It is what we call knowledge in common parlance. Knowledge is more than just information. Knowledge knows inner connections between units of information. Knowledge is holistic.

In Vedic science, students are always advised to think through for themselves the knowledge (Pramana = information) they have learned from a teacher. In this way, the inner connections between the information items are established and it becomes Jnana, i.e. interconnected knowledge.

A database becomes a knowledge base when everything is related to everything else. The data is then processed, digested, so to speak. It is no longer just information in its raw state, where it is just accumulated and put on a big pile. In the knowledge base, it is known how the data items relate to each other. As soon as I create a table of contents for a database or generate an index file, the database moves towards a knowledge base. For a good knowledge base this goes much further. The goal is to recognize and understand all internal relationships. Such a knowledge base in our Brain Software is what the Yoga Sutras call Jnana.

There is a third level of knowledge. This knowledge is called Prajna. In Sanskrit, the meaning of a word can always be inferred from its component parts. For Prajna, this means that we can divide it into the syllables pra and jna. Pra is a prefix and means something that exists before or that is more basic. It corresponds to the Latin prefix pre. As it was said, almost all languages are derived from Sanskrit.

Jna is the word root of Jnana, the general concept of knowledge. Then what is pra-jna? It is that which comes before knowledge. It is the knowledge from the original source. This is a knowledge which is not only interconnected but, moreover, is imbued with infinity. Whoever experiences infinity in his consciousness has access to Prajna knowledge.

Prajna is perfect knowledge. It carries truth within itself. Therefore, it is called 'ritam bhara prajna'. Ritam is truth, Bhara means to carry and Prajna is just this infinite knowledge.

Prajna includes all the huge amounts of information of the universe computer, which are big but still limited; then it is additionally networked, so it knows all the inner connections and additionally it is also imbued with infinity.

Infinity as the real and experiential ultimate reality also has the name 'Sat-Cit-Ananda'. These are the three basic properties of the ultimate reality, which actually appears as perfect silence without properties. Sat is truth, that which is real. Cit is pure consciousness and Ananda is happiness.

3. The Field of all Knowledge

Prajna knowledge is always permeated by the infinity of Sat-Cit-Ananda. Because Sat is the ultimate reality, Prajna is the true knowledge. Truth means that which is actual. It agrees with the actual situation at all levels, at the level of infinity, the level of interconnected knowledge, and even at the level of information.

Samadhi is the Sanskrit word for the experience of the infinity of Sat-Cit-Ananda. In this experience, Sat-Cit-Ananda is reflected in the individual Brain Software of a person. It is like the reflection of the Sun on a water surface. If the reflecting surface is completely without ripples, then the reflection is perfect. The more turbulent the ripples, the more distorted the reflection. The ripples are the thought processes in the Brain Software. They have to be calmed down so that the clear, pure knowledge (Prajna) can be recognized.

Pure knowledge accompanied by the infinity of Samadhi experience is the calmest kind of wave in the Brain Software. It least disturbs the reflection of Sat-Cit-Ananda. Therefore, the qualities of Sat-Cit-Ananda come out best in pure knowledge. That is, pure knowledge carries within it truth (Sat), pure consciousness (Cit) and happiness (Ananda). In addition also infinity (Ananta).

From the various Sanskrit terms for knowledge, a hierarchy of knowledge emerges:
- Pure Consciousness (Sat-Cit-Ananda, Ananta) →
- Pure Knowledge (Prajna) →
- Knowledge (Jnana) →
- Information (Pramana)

Thus, the field of all knowledge is thoroughly explained.

4. Magic or Technology?

How would our ancestors 250 years ago have viewed a light bulb that we can now so easily turn on and off with a switch? It would have been magic to them. For us, it is merely technology.

So, what makes the difference between magic and technology? It is not the age, but our knowledge that makes the difference. We are used to simply flipping a light switch and having the light come on. It has become normal everyday life for us.

To switch on an incandescent lamp or an LED lamp, we don't need to understand how the technology works in detail or how these light sources are manufactured. For us, it's a technology if it works reliably.

How would our ancestors have reacted to incandescent lamps or LEDs? They would never have seen anything like it before and would have been startled at first. Depending on the circumstances and the time period, they would have reacted differently to this initial shock.

What special thing is this that produces light without fire? Shortly before the discovery of the electric filament in 1801 by Louis Jacques Thénard, one would have guessed that it was a new invention. The battery had been invented by Alessandro Volta a year earlier. With it, it had become possible to conduct a current through a metal wire and make it glow.

Much earlier, however, one would not have admired this new light-generating thing so much as an invention, but the fear would have been excessive. What one does not understand and does not know would then simply be a magic which instils fear. But it only does that for the person who doesn't know the magic. We would all have been magicians then, since we can make light without fire. To do that, we use this little magic thing called a light switch.

How would one have dealt with the magicians who had mastered such light magic? Depending on the time epoch quite differently. In the

4. Magic or Technology?

deepest Middle Ages one would have found apparently religious reasons to eliminate the magicians or witches. In reality, however, it was never the commandment of any religion to kill people. Quite the contrary. It was the hidden primal fears of people that came to the fore. In addition, however, there were also claims to power by institutionalized religious leaders. This is how the atrocities of the Middle Ages against people with special knowledge came about.

In ancient times, however, we all would have had a good chance that our LEDs would not have been called magic, but instead miracles. We might then have gone down in history as saints, or perhaps as the founders of a new religion of light, or even as gods who came to Earth in flying ships to bring light to mankind.

If today, by studying Vedic science and modern science, and especially computer science, I have a much more accurate classification of knowledge and information, both in the brain and in the universe as a whole, I do not want to be called a magician or a saint for that. It is simply a technology. Not even a new technology, but an ancient technology from earlier, more luminous times that I have rediscovered! This technology has magic in the sense of a fascination that comes from it (more on that in the last chapter). However, it need not inspire fear. By seeing the technology, I have calmed my fear and can use the magic of knowledge completely naturally.

In the meantime it has become a knowledge of physics that there must be an information field which influences everything. From this knowledge we came to the universe computer (see chapter 2). Thinking a little further, we will then come to the knower of this computer. More about this in the next chapter.

5. The Knowledge of the Omniscient

In this chapter I would like to explain the words 'karpūragauraṁ' from the introductory verse. Karpura is camphor, an intense smelling white substance distilled from the essential oils of the camphor tree, which is highly inflammable. Gauram is the colour white. The cover of this book shows a camphor flame as it is often used in India in ceremonies such as Yagyas or Pujas.

What is so special about camphor? What is so special about the colour white? Both terms symbolize complete knowledge. I would like to explain this in more detail in this chapter.

Camphor is a solid at room temperature. It is highly flammable. When we ignite it, it immediately burns intensely with a high flame. It is in all known forms of matter (states of aggregation) at the same time. It is solid, at least the part that is not yet burning. Through the heat of the flame, however, it also melts and is liquid on its surface. At the same time, it evaporates and is thus gaseous. The gaseous camphor combines with the oxygen in the air and becomes the luminous plasma of the flame. In the black soot produced by combustion, large quantities of perfectly regular C_{60} balls are formed.[5] They consist of exactly 60 carbon atoms and look like the smallest football we know. They symbolize the inner order of space.

Thus, camphor exists in all five forms of matter simultaneously and symbolizes a complete knowledge of matter.[6] The light and heat emitted by a camphor flame symbolize knowledge of energy.

---

[5] The C_{60} balls are also called Bucky balls or fullerenes in honour of their discoverer Buckminster Fuller.
[6] Empty space is of course not a form of matter and its internal order is only symbolically represented by the C_{60} balls.

5. The Knowledge of the Omniscient

The C_{60} balls also have a positive effect on health. They strengthen the immune system. Therefore, the ancient Indian custom of stroking your hands over a camphor flame and touching your face with the fine soot on your hands is a very useful and intelligent exercise. This strengthens the immune system and helps to prevent diseases.

The word 'gauraṁ' from the opening verse is the colour white. 'Karpūra gauraṁ' means white like camphor. Now natural camphor is sometimes slightly yellowish or reddish in colour. Thus, a light yellow or a light red or pink is also called 'gauraṁ'. The purer the distillation process of the camphor oil from the camphor trees, the more the camphor becomes really white.

Thus, the word Gauram is a symbol of purity. In the pure form it is white, in the slightly mixed form it is yellowish or reddish. Knowledge can also be in different degrees of purity.

The colour white is composed of all the colours of the rainbow. Through a crystal, the white can be fanned out to form a rainbow (spectrum). If the colours yellow or red dominate, this rainbow is not uniform. Only with white is it even and forms a full spectrum. Thus, the colour white, like camphor, symbolizes a complete knowledge, a pure knowledge without contamination.

Arguably the most important property of knowledge is its perfection. Knowledge is the more perfect, the more it corresponds to the actual reality. Now, if any property can be measured, then there must necessarily be persons or beings who possess more of it than others. So there must also be someone who possesses the most of that quality.

This person the Yoga Sutras refer to as Ishvara. 'Ish' is the ruler and 'vara' is the best. So it is the best ruler. The Yoga Sutras say that the best ruler knows everything and that there can be only one who fits this description.

To know everything is, in fact, to know everything at all levels of knowledge. This knowledge is complete. It includes all the information of the universe computer (Pramana), all the networked knowledge

(Jnana), all the knowledge pervaded by infinity (Prajna), and pure consciousness (Sat-Cit-Ananda). See Chapter 3 (The Field of All Knowledge).

This complete knowledge is a characteristic of Ishvara. Therefore, we also call him the omniscient. His knowledge is at once nuanced and infinite. He knows every elementary particle in the universe, the entire history of everything since the beginning of time, simultaneously all interrelationships, and simultaneously eternity and the relationship between time and eternity. This is the knowledge of the Omniscient.

This knowledge of Ishvara encompasses the entire material and energetic world, that is, the entire objective world, in addition to the entire subjective world. Thus, Ishvara knows the entire universe, all its inhabitants, every galaxy, every sun, every planet, every moon, every plant, every animal, every stone, every grain of sand, every drop of water, every molecule, every elementary particle, every ray of light, every field, every human being, every spiritual being, every thought of every human being at all times.

He knows everything since the beginning of the universe. And he knows everything on each of the four levels of knowledge as explained in Chapter 3. His store of information is the universe computer, but he knows more than that, for the universe computer functions according to his program.

Its sub-programs are the Laws of Nature. The most important are the programs of creation, conservation, and rest, the program of organizing power, the program of life, and the program of emanation.

Ishvara knows more than any of his subroutines. Ishvara's knowledge is perfect. It knows every detail and at the same time the holistic whole, knows all the connections and the wholeness. Ishvara knows the objective universe, the subjective universe and the Self of everything. This is the knowledge of the Omniscient.

6. The Function of an Avatar

With so much knowledge of Ishvara, we as humans could almost despair, if it were not for the Avatar. The knowledge of Ishvara is so incomprehensible for us humans that we can only do something with a tiny part of it. To know everything about everything in the universe would completely overload our little brains.

So what does Ishvara do to share his knowledge with us? He enables us to communicate through his Avatars. The function of an Avatar is described by the words 'karuṇāvatāraṁ' in our opening verse. 'Karuṇā' means compassion. 'Avatāraṁ' means the embodiment of the omniscient.

Why does the Omniscient One incarnate? [7] Because he feels compassion for us. He knows our often-hopeless situation. No one can push him into anything, no one is above him. But out of compassion he helps us. Since he knows everything, he also knows all our thoughts. Always! Then why doesn't he always help us? Because we are allowed to choose it ourselves, if and how much we want to accept his help.

I would like to describe this situation with a process that you have probably all experienced before. A fly has lost its way in a room and desperately wants to get back into the fresh air and continue its journey through the great outdoors. What does it do? It flies into a window pane and hits its head massively. It may stagger a bit or even need to rest for a while and knowing nothing better, it repeats the same painful action over and over again.

---

[7] I think the gender craze is inappropriate, especially here. When I speak of Ishvara as 'Him', I equally mean His feminine expression as well. He is above that kind of duality. He can appear male or female. But I don't like to call him an 'It' because that is also considered cute, childish, even passive. It would describe him even more inappropriately.

Find Your Personal Avatar

The fly knows from all its experience of life that if it sees nature before it and does not recognise any obstacles, then it must be able to fly there. The law of nature that things like a pane of glass can be completely transparent and still hold back, it does not know this law of nature. It does not see the slight reflections by which we recognize a pane of glass. So it doesn't include this law of nature in its considerations and keeps banging against the pane until finally, perhaps after days, it dies of hunger, thirst and exhaustion.

When we watch the fly, it is perfectly clear to us why it is unsuccessful. Instead of flying out through an open window, it keeps banging against the glass pane, through which it simply cannot fly. But then when we try to help it escape, it gets scared and avoids any attempt to help. This can go on for quite a while until it has hidden itself so well that we can't help it any more with the best will in the world and then often give up in annoyance. What does the fly do wrong? It misjudges the situation and does not accept our help.

What are we doing wrong by not accepting the help of Ishvara? The same as the poor fly. The help is offered again and again, but also rejected again and again. This help comes from compassion. That is the meaning of 'karuṇā'.

And how does the help come to us? Through the Avatar. So the Avatar who meets us or talks to us is the expression of the ongoing compassion of Ishvara, the All-Knowing. Ishvara has given us free will, and He has no need to secretly take that free will away from us. Therefore, he does not impose his help on us, but we are free to choose whether we want his help.

If you dear reader do not believe in free will, then just assume that you are reading this book now out of predestination and will also follow the recommendations in this book out of predestination. You will do well with it!

The Avatar can help us get out of any predicament. He or she can be male or female, or neither. He or she has access to all knowledge that

6. The Function of an Avatar

exists, knows the same knowledge as Ishvara. But he filters this knowledge for us in such a way that we can still process it and do something with it.

The knowledge from our personal Avatar then comes as words, sentences, a normal conversation or as pictures or as feelings. The Avatar can communicate with us in a multimedia way. It doesn't have to be all internal. Ishvara also loves to show that he is in control of the whole universe. So his communication can come from the environment as well. He plays on all instruments simultaneously.

Unsolved problems only come about because we do not know a solution, at least not a solution that we can practically apply. Thus, problems come about through lack of knowledge. With access to all knowledge, we can solve all our problems. The Avatar can give us that access and is the living compassion of the All-Knowing for us and our situation.

Let's just accept his help and enjoy our life in joy and happiness! Problems will quickly diminish; our wisdom will grow and access to the source of infinite creativity will open more and more. The meaning of life will be achieved. Our consciousness will turn to the Omniscient and will come to the highest possible level. As we come closer to the light, the light will illuminate every dark corner and problems will disappear.

Moreover, our creativity will also increase. Ishvara is not only the best problem solver but also the greatest inspiration. Good opportunities will come more frequently and will also be recognized as such by us.

Ishvara is not only omniscient, but also omnipotent. With such an all-knowing friend, or such an all-powerful friend, there is nothing that we cannot achieve. Anything is possible!

Our Avatar enables us to have this connection to all knowledge and power, and will tirelessly assist us in the positive development of our lives. That is its function.

7. How Many Avatars are There?

Our universe consists of a hundred billion galaxies and each of these galaxies also has about a hundred billion stars, most of them even bigger and brighter than our Sun. Anyone here who can only imagine that humans are the only intelligent life form in the universe may be somewhat handicapped in their ability to think. Whether this handicap comes from a lack of or one-sided education, or from strict beliefs, we can put aside.

We can assume with great certainty that the entire universe is filled with life of various forms. Many of these life forms will be highly intelligent. Many will have a level of technological development far in advance of our own. After all, our technological development didn't really begin until Rennaisance about 400 years ago. Then science began its systematic experiments. Galileo Galilei began to measure the speed at which bodies fall with simple clocks.

It is very likely, due to the sheer size of the universe, that a multitude of intelligent life forms will precede us not only by hundreds, but by thousands, perhaps even millions of years. This refers to their overall technological development and especially their abilities to travel through the universe. Far more fascinating, however, would be the probable higher development of their consciousness.

The Omniscient One, after all, overlooks everything in our universe. How will he react to these many different forms of life? He will send Avatars to the various suns and planets and moons who can understand the species and communicate with them in the best possible way.

On a planet whose surface is completely covered with water, an Avatar might appear as a dolphin, able to converse with the other intelligent dolphins. On a planet or moon where mostly dinosaurs live, he will appear as a dinosaur. On a hot fire star, he may appear as a fire

7. How Many Avatars are There?

creature. As I said before, Infinity is also infinitely playful and knows and masters all forms of matter, all elements, all forms of energy.

How many Avatars have there been on Earth? A great many! Many more than we know of from Western history. More than the founders of the religions still practiced today. Western historiography has forgotten almost everything that goes back more than 6,000 years. Vedic - literature, on the other hand, goes back much further. It measures ages in millions of years. In these long periods of time there were many more Avatars than we know from today's religions. Vedic literature enumerates many of them. There are hundreds whose names are still known today.

Some religions insist that no one should make an image of the All-knowing and Almighty. This makes a lot of sense, because who could correctly represent infinity in a finite image? There are, however, other religions which, although they are also unable to capture the One All-Knowing in a picture, are by no means afraid to depict the various levels of Avatars.

If we look at the latest findings in physics, there is much to suggest that our universe exists in an information field, that is as old as the universe and as new as the shortest time. It is as vast as the universe and as intricate as its smallest spatial unit. I call this information field the universe computer, which I described in Chapter 2.

Then what is our universe actually? Actually, it is information. This information has arisen from infinite, pure knowledge. This is the knowledge of the All-Knowing. Pure consciousness is the basis of infinite knowledge.

Thus we have a sequence and a hierarchy of how creation arises. It begins with pure consciousness.

- Pure Consciousness →
- Pure knowledge →
- Knowledge →

Find Your Personal Avatar

- Information →
- Space →
- Energy →
- Matter.

From the complete, infinite, pure knowledge in pure consciousness, Ishvara, the Omniscient, overlooks all that exists. He knows all the software and hardware of the universe computer. Thus he also controls everything that exists and creates different levels of Avatars. All these are actually only levels of knowledge and information in the universe computer.

At the highest level of the Avatars, Ishvara creates for himself the laws of nature, first the basic ones, then the ones based on them. The vedic literature describes them as groups and families of so-called devas. Devas is sometimes translated as gods. The term natural laws, however, is more accurate. There are many of them, while Ishvara exists only as the One. The Devas are the most important programs running in the universe computer. They control all processes in the universe, whereby Ishvara always controls the highest level, as he is the best ruler.

When an Avatar appears on Earth as a human being, he or she is an incarnation (a descent) of these Devas and thus always an incarnation of Ishvara. So the Avatar is not a second, separate person, but he is Ishvara in a special form. Ishvara is infinitely adaptable and can appear in infinite varieties.

An Avatar can be born and live with a body, but he can also appear purely mentally. With a mental Avatar, who can contact the Brain Software of any human being, it is possible to experience the direct connection to Ishvara.

There are an unlimited number of these Avatars. I call them the personal Avatars. More about this in the next chapter.

8. The Personal Avatar

The personal Avatar is described in our opening verse by the name 'bhavaṁ bhavānī'. Who is Bhavaṁ? He is an Avatar of Ishvara at the first level of hierarchy. He is responsible for returning any activity to its resting state. When an atom falls back from an excited state to the resting state with the lowest energy, it is Bhavaṁ who causes this to happen. More precisely, it is Bhavānī who brings it about along with Bhavaṁ. This is true not only of atoms, but of all systems in the universe. Every system has the basic tendency to go to its most tranquil state as soon as it gets the opportunity. Bhavaṁ and Bhavānī bring it to rest. They are the natural laws of rest. They are the programs in the universe computer that can calm everything. They are always taking effect everywhere.

Bhavaṁ is the male principle, Bhavānī is the female principle. Bhavaṁ is pure knowledge, Bhavānī is the organizing power inherent in pure knowledge. They work together. They are also called Shiva and Shakti. Shiva (Bhavaṁ) represents pure knowledge, Shakti (Bhavānī) its organizing power.

When we find peace in a beautiful meditation, it is Shiva and Shakti who enable us to do so. Both are special forms of Ishvara. They are the first Avatars who diminish activity and enhance stillness. They know the infinite silence of pure consciousness. Shiva and Shakti are the essence of our personal Avatars.

Although some Avatars are universally known, they still appear to each person in a personal way. Consider Jesus, for example. While he was a historical figure some 2000 years ago, he still functions as a mental Avatar today. For many people, he is a mental access point to the Omniscient and Almighty. No one alive today has met Jesus personally, at least not with his body existing now. It is similar in other religions. The human bodies of the religion's founders or God-figures have all long since passed away. They exist only as mental Avatars.

Exceptions are natural religions, which have natural phenomena as access to the omniscient and omnipotent, for example a living fire with which someone can communicate. This fire exists as a perceptible reality and not only mentally.

In the Veda and Vedic literature, Agni is a law of nature and an Avatar. He is often interpreted as the god of fire. In reality, he is the natural law that controls energy in any form. Energy behaves in a predictable manner. This behaviour is the stable character of Agni. At the same time, fire is also playful. In firewood it goes sometimes here and sometimes there, crackles sometimes here and throws sparks there. Agni has a playful character, while he is also powerful and can grow to any size.

Agni is called the mediator between the gods (the supreme Avatars) and human beings. He is a living Avatar. Like all Avatars, he is an expression of Ishvara, the best ruler. The Upanishads tell of someone who became enlightened simply by communicating with sacrificial fires. That is how powerful the Avatar Agni can be!

Now let's take a closer look at the personal, human Avatars, for example Jesus. Does he appear to each person in the same way? Not at all! Each and every one experience him in the way they can, based on their knowledge and personal experience. Therefore, there are as many variations of Jesus as there are worshippers of Jesus. Jesus adapts himself to us personally so that we can develop a personal relationship with him. Thus, Jesus becomes a personal Avatar. This does not mean that Jesus takes on our weaknesses. He remains at His high level of purity and perfection and yet He allows us to relate to Him and in this way gain access to the Omniscient One.

The same is true for all Avatars. They adapt themselves in such a way that they form the optimal bridge for a person to the infinity of the Omniscient. A personal Avatar does not have to have any relation to known Avatars from the history of the world.

The Avatar is the Bridge to the Infinity of Pure Consciousness. He is the Bridge to the Omniscient. That is his essential quality. The other

8. The Personal Avatar

qualities he adapts to give us good access to the All-Knowing. This means that an Avatar can appear both male and female, or genderless.

An Avatar can appear in female form. In most cases, it is a mother figure. The divine Mother appears to us in an infinite number of forms. Whether women or men are more important does not matter. The Avatar appears in the way that is easiest for the person.

Is the mental Avatar just a figment of your imagination? No! Definitely not, because the knowledge we get through the Avatar we can verify. We will see that it is real when we have learned to communicate properly, when we have removed blockages, thought patterns, beliefs, etc. that block a good flow of communication. More on this later in Chapter 13 (Neutralizing Disturbances).

The advantages of communication with the personal Avatar are immeasurable. By communication I don't mean a one-way prayer, but a living communication, an inner dialogue. The Avatar gives profound, meaningful answers. The inner dialogue is not a one-sided plea and supplication as in a prayer, which does not work well anyway.

Repeated supplication comes with a great misunderstanding, that is, that Ishvara would not know our every thought immediately. He knows everything, including every thought. When we understand this, we approach communication with Ishvara very differently.

An Avatar can help us communicate with Ishvara in many ways. This communication is life-changing and infinitely valuable. Yet it must be done in a workable way so that we can succeed at all times. This is why the personal Avatar is so important. So let's set out to find our personal Avatar!

9. How do I Find my Avatar?

Dear reader, surely you have already noticed your so-called inner voice. Unfortunately, most people pay too little attention to their inner voice. It is our own voice and yet it conveys something new to us. We can learn to discover it as our access to Ishvara. We can find our personal Avatar by learning to listen to our inner voice.

Our Avatar will not appear as a holographic projection in the sky to manipulate the masses of people with alien voices in their heads. If that ever comes, don't fall for it. Our inner voice is not a technological mind manipulation.

How often have you said to yourself, if only I had listened to my inner voice, my intuition, then I would have done everything right! Who does not know this? Our intuition advises us to do something in a certain way, to refrain from doing something else. We don't listen to it and then later realize we made a mistake. So why not listen to intuition more often? It can be learned and trained.

Often we lack the confidence to do this. We didn't learn anything about intuition at school. It was not a school subject. Yet it exists and people who have learned to trust their intuition go through life more easily. There are numerous books that prove that all great business people became great because they trusted their intuition. Intuition gives us the right knowledge at the right time. It is an access to Ishvara, the All-Knowing.

Maybe you experience your intuition more as random thoughts. Sometimes I have an intuition and often I have none. It doesn't have to stay that way, because intuition can be systematically developed and expanded into a dialogue. This is the inner dialogue with our Avatar. It can take place in different ways, on the level of feelings, of images, and most simply as a direct, inner conversation.

How do I come to this inner dialogue? Through trust, through openness, through devotion to the All-Knowing, to Ishvara. Trust that he is

9. How do I Find my Avatar?

completely positive towards me and will help me in every way. Openness, because I know that he already knows my every thought and that I can open myself to him in every way. Devotion, because my heart flows with love for him and becomes more and more alive, refreshing my whole life.

At the beginning of this process, there is often some resistance to overcome. I see this over and over again in the personal trainings I've given to hundreds of people to learn how to communicate with their Avatar and practice it in a simple way in their daily lives. I call these short 1-day coaching sessions the Intuition Training of the Brain Software. What changes in the Brain Software? Version 6 of the Brain Software, the intuition version, is installed. It is also called God Consciousness. It brings a completely different view of the world.

Those who have studied the subject of higher states of consciousness know how many years, decades or whole lifetimes, such a development has taken. Nevertheless, nothing is impossible for Ishvara and with the right knowledge the great transformation to God Consciousness can be realized in one day.

What resistance is there to overcome? Often there are doubts as to whether such a dialogue can be genuine or doubts as to whether it can be done properly, whether it can be done so quickly or whether it can succeed at all. Then there are a number of beliefs or thought patterns to overcome. I will write more about these topics in chapter 13 (Neutralizing Disturbances).

But all this can be easily overcome, and eventually our personal Avatar enters our lives. We do not have to do any work for this. Devotion to the Omniscient One is enough. The rest is done by the Almighty. She is the female form of Ishvara. She can do anything. She creates the right Avatar for us, with whom we can optimally communicate. Male or female, younger or older or the same age, our Avatar has exactly the qualities we need for optimal communication. The Almighty can do anything and creates the right Avatar for us. So we can start this life-enhancing communication and do it forever, and make our lives infinitely better.

10. An Eternal Relationship

Why should I rely on an inner voice? It could be anything. Who can guarantee me that I'm really doing well with it? Does my inner voice really come from my Avatar or perhaps from a completely different source? Haven't there always been people who were completely misguided by their supposed inner voices? Almost everyone who comes into contact with their intuition or inner voice for the first time has questions like these.

The answer to these questions is again in our opening verse. The word 'sadā' describes the relationship with Ishvara through our personal Avatar. It means eternal. The relationship with the Omniscient is eternal, so it is without beginning and without end. We can rely on Ishvara, the Omniscient. He will never leave us.

Ishvara is eternal and we are eternal. Our relationship is also eternal. What do I mean, we are eternal? Don't we have a body that was born and will die someday? Yes, we do, but that's not who we are. The body is like a garment we put on. We have covered our real essence, that is, what we really are, with the body. When a piece of clothing is damaged and no longer usable, we simply change it.

Once I realize who I really am, then I know my immortality. Bodies come and go, but I remain constantly. Since the Omniscient One is also constant, my relationship with Him is constant. A constant relationship is intense. It is strong. From my relationship with him I draw infinite strength.

Which people are still interested in me once my body has grown old? Actually, no one anymore. The children are perhaps out of the house and live their own lives. Maybe the partner is still there, maybe not, maybe you don't have much to say to each other anymore. With age, friends disappear, perhaps because they have already left the Earth, perhaps because they live somewhere else or have found other interests or are no longer quite there mentally.

10. An Eternal Relationship

Who cares about me then? The one, the all-knowing! For he does not see me essentially as a body. He can give me a new body. He is always interested in developing my knowledge and consciousness. He is and remains interested in me as an eternally existing being. That is a stable and eternal relationship.

Once you realize this, you would be foolish not to cultivate the relationship with the All-Knowing. How do we cultivate this relationship? Like any other relationship, through our attention! Our constant source of happiness and wisdom within us is enlivened by our attention.

So let us turn to the Omniscient, let Him come into our lives constantly and spread His beneficial influence over us. Then we will be all right. Our development of consciousness will take a tremendous leap forward.

Then our lives will no longer be determined by karma. Then all good will no longer be rewarded with good and bad punished with bad. The Omniscient and Omnipotent can balance our karmic debts. He can erase the karmic memories in the universe computer. He has this power. We do not have to laboriously work off our karma. It's hopeless anyway. In thousands of lifetimes we have not succeeded in paying off our karmic debts, because in most lifetimes much more new karma has been added.

Entire religions have adapted to this vale of suffering. Some see suffering, others karma as God-given. Those who see only this have actually lost most of their connection to the divine infinite source of happiness and wisdom. How do we get back to our source? How does it work practically?

11. At Eye Level

Ishvara, the best ruler, would have the power to leave us eternally in this up and down of karma. With our good deeds we have earned the good, with our bad deeds the bad. Yes, there are laws of nature that accurately manage karma. The universe computer can calculate very precisely!

But then there is also compassion, the word karuṇā from our opening verse. How does it show itself practically in our lives? Through another word from the verse, through vasantaṁ. This Sanskrit word means 'the dwellers'. By this are meant Shiva and Shakti. They are the Avatars of heavenly silence.

Where do they live? In us! As Avatars. So they don't just stay in their celestial realms, they come directly to us. They come as close to us as is even possible. They live in us. They come to us as human beings. They come at eye level. They appear to us as personal Avatars. So they take on closely the character that we feel comfortable communicating with.

With this we can address them directly as human beings. This is the infinite compassion of Ishvara. He presents himself to us in human form, capable of human communication. At the same time he does not need to hover always a meter above us, but he comes at eye level. We can communicate directly with him because he dwells within us.

He dwells within us in a human form as man or woman, or as both combined. What is the advantage of this human form and this human character that comes with it? The advantage is that we already know how to communicate with a human being. This is exactly the kind of communication we can have with our Avatar.

When people in some religions throw themselves in the dust before their God or always look upwards, they make a mistake. They separate themselves from their beloved. They create a separation and often they are no longer able to overcome this self-created separation.

11. At Eye Level

They have, so to speak, pushed their God away upwards. Off to heaven! There he shall remain, and there he remains, still seeing everything and not bothering us any further. And man continues to prostrate himself outwardly before his God, whom at the same time he keeps at a distance inwardly. That is a nonsensical way of proceeding!

It all goes much better with a personal Avatar. He comes at eye level. Now communication is very easy. The Avatar is not below me and not above me. He has a human character.

What does that mean practically? It means that I can meet my Avatar, that I can get to know him or her better and better. It means that I recognize him or her immediately, that I maintain an inner dialogue. It means that I let him or her or both participate in my life.

The Avatar then becomes like a good friend or relative. He is interested in everything that interests me. He gives his comments on my actions, plans, ideas, thoughts, feelings. He answers my questions. He is an inexhaustible source of wisdom. After all, He knows me inside and out. I don't need to hide anything. We are such good friends that we can talk about absolutely anything.

The Yoga Sutra 1.23 says, "Or by attention to Ishvara (is attained Samadhi)." Samadhi is this absolutely tranquil consciousness. So the sutra says that attention to Ishvara brings us into this infinitely deep tranquility. How does that happen?

Ishvara knows all thoughts and therefore always notices our attention to him. Then he bends down to us. This is done by appearing to us as an Avatar. The first form of each Avatar are Shiva and Shakti, the Avatars of tranquillity. They take us deeper and deeper into the absolute tranquility of Samadhi. Then Ishvara bends down even further towards us until he comes to eye level. He appears to us as a human being. That is our personal Avatar. With him we have our joy.

Joy, awareness, and truth are the qualities of infinite, pure consciousness. Our Avatar takes us there quickly. Where exactly does he live?

12. Where does my Avatar Live?

Imagine that a very dear relative, a friend or a girlfriend comes to your home for a visit. He or she has already done so much good for you, has often given you abundant gifts, always listened to you, always given you good advice with which you could really solve your problems. He or she has inspired you, built you up, boosted your confidence. Now he or she comes to visit. How do you treat them?

You treat them like a good guest. You greet them warmly, let them come in, show them around, serve them refreshments, let them freshen up themselves, offer them a comfortable place to sit, serve them food and drink, entertain them, and talk to them at length. These are the rules of good hospitality that are practiced in countries with ancient advanced civilizations even today. In India, there is a simple rule of hospitality. You treat the guest like God.

Now imagine that your guest is actually God and wants to dwell with you. As the Avatar, the Omniscient and the Almighty want to stay with you in your body. Which room do you offer?

Of course, you offer the best room. You want your guest to feel comfortable. That way, they'll stay forever and you'll feel good about it, too. The best room in our body is our heart. It connects the whole body through the blood vessels and constantly nourishes it with our blood. Our heart is the appropriate place for our Avatar. It is also where we can perceive our higher self and where we can converse with our Avatar.

Our opening verse says in the line 'sadāvasantaṁ hṛdayāravinde' ... You are always dwelling in the lotus of my heart. Hṛdaya is the heart. Aravinde is lotus. Why Vedic literature calls the heart a lotus? Because, firstly, it is in the form of a closed lotus flower, hanging in the lake of the chest by the great veins, just like a lotus bud hanging on a thick stalk. On the other hand, the lotus is also the Vedic symbol of wholeness, which is found in each individual leaf. Each leaf of the lotus has the shape of the whole lotus. Therefore, the lotus embodies the holistic principle.

12. Where does my Avatar Live?

The Lotus of the Heart is the proper room we offer our Avatar. There he dwells forever. Shiva and Shakti, the pure knowledge and its organizing power work from our heart, enlivening our whole body, including our brain, and bringing our Brain Software to the highest level of development.

We do not have photos of the well-known Avatars of the world religions, but only painted pictures, drawings or figures. Your Avatar need not appear to you like the drawings of Shiva and Shakti. It can look like the drawing of a religious founder close to you, such as Jesus, Buddha, Krishna, or Kuan Yin. But he can also just communicate with you verbally.

You don't have to make a picture of your personal Avatar. Those who worship the Prophet Muhammad should not make a picture of him. Then don't make a picture either, but communicate with him in words and feelings. From verbal communication you will come to know your Avatar better and better.

How do you treat your personal Avatar in your heart? You pay a lot of attention to him. That way, he can be a blessing in your life. He will always give you the best advice. But he leaves it up to you whether you follow his advice.

If you follow them, you will gradually get better and better. Many things will work out better. You will have new ideas, you will be able to solve old problems, you will be able to realize your wishes. Everything in your life will change for the better if you take up the suggestions of your personal Avatar and put them into practice. Your happiness will increase more and more. Already after a short time you will live in Heaven on Earth!

13. Neutralize Interference

Why haven't you always lived in Heaven on Earth? What has prevented you from doing so in your past and perhaps even today? There are a number of disturbances, and we will now take a closer look at them. They all have to do with various forms of ignorance.

These ignorances are expressed in our opening verse by the word 'bhujagendra'. It is composed of 'bhujaga' and 'indra'. The 'a' at the end of the word and the 'i' at the beginning of the next word merge into one 'e'.[8] Bhujaga is a snake. Indra is a king. Bhujagendra is the king of snakes. This is the epitome of ignorance and all the dangers it brings.

The snake is also the symbol of the kundalini force, which is awakened and rises in our spine from the very bottom to the very top, from the rump[9] to the brain. As long as it is perceived as moving, like a snake, it can create a certain fear. But this is the ignorant way of looking at Kundalini. In reality it is not a snake but a rope. There is no danger from the rope. It corresponds to the nerve strands in our spinal cord.

From a broader perspective, however, the snake is also a symbol of every kind of ignorance. It results from a false view of the world. This gives rise to perceived dangers and corresponding fears. These include thought patterns, beliefs, emotional patterns, blocks, traumas, impressions, illusions and the like. They are all the result of ignorance, and they are all eliminated when ignorance is eliminated.

So how can we neutralize this interference? It's simple! Our Avatar does it for us. How does he do it? Playfully easy! He hangs the snake around His neck like a garland. Our opening verse spells it out with the word 'bhujagendrahāram'. The 'hāram' is a garland. The dangerous king of snakes with all his venom, his art of lying, his power of deception cannot defeat our Avatar but is easily defeated by him playfully. Finally,

---
[8] This 'e' is pronounced like in 'set' or 'let'.
[9] Actually, from the Coccyx.

13. Neutralize Interference

he hangs as a decoration on the neck of our Avatar. This picture also means that the Kundalini power has risen.

With the constant support of our personal Avatar, this all happens very quickly. With his support, there is no long, dark night of the soul. When we communicate with our Avatar, we have the full power of the universe computer at our disposal. In an instant, all these disturbances are neutralized.

What used to seem like an insurmountable karma that we might have been working on for many lifetimes now becomes a small thing. Our Avatar can do it all for us. After all, the entire university is embedded in the universe computer. Clearing some personal karmic memory is a small thing for Ishvara. So the blocks disappear and our heart, brain and nervous system purify themselves on a material and energetic level. At the same time, the corresponding malware programs are deleted on the information level.

Where does all the karma go? It hangs as a garland on our Avatar's neck. So no one else needs to be harmed with it. We don't need to keep passing on our disturbances and blockages and negative energies to others. Our Avatar simply makes them harmless and has fun doing it.

How do we remove the blockages concretely? We talk about it with our Avatar. In all openness! We open our hearts. Yes, we may pour out our whole heart to our Avatar. No secrets, no matter how intimate, are left out. Whatever the topic is at the moment, it will be put in order and cleansed.

In this way it becomes easier and easier for us to dive into the deep silence of Samadhi and from there to experience the whole world with serenity and infinite joy in our hearts.

14. Achieve Everything

Where is the journey going? Our Avatar accompanies us to ever higher levels of happiness, to ever higher consciousness. The attention to Ishvara that we constantly cultivate through our Avatar brings our consciousness to deeper and deeper rest, to intense Samadhi.

Samadhi is the basis for experiencing extraordinary abilities. With Samadhi, our attention becomes a precise instrument, a tool with which we can achieve anything. These abilities are also called Siddhi. There are two types of Siddhis, the knowledge Siddhis and the power Siddhis. With the knowledge Siddhis we can get all knowledge from Shiva. With the power Siddhis we can attain everything through Shakti.

The Siddhis lead to liberation. They lead from attachment to liberation. When we focus our attention on something, it is still an attachment to the object of our attention. When the result of the Siddhi appears in Samadhi, that is, in infinite tranquillity, it is a liberation because the experience is permeated with infinity. Actually, it is then no longer an experience but only our infinite Self which appears in the form of the Siddhi result.

Patanjali has described the Siddhi methods in detail in chapter 3 of his Yoga Sutras. He clearly shows how the path from attachment to liberation takes place. What the Siddhis do, I quote here most simply from my book 'Brain Software' (from p. 258):

"The yogi[10] realizes his infinite Self in every place of his attention and thus overcomes all limits of his perception, his cognitive faculty and his sphere of influence. This even goes so far that he can overcome the bondage of natural laws. His ability to perceive is no longer bound by the limitations of his sense organs of his body. He can perceive hidden and far distant things, that is, he can see, hear, touch, etc. He can see into the past and the future, travel through the universe with his attention,

---

[10] This, of course, again refers to both male and female yogis.

14. Achieve Everything

observe the finest components of the world, even smaller than atoms. All the limitations of his perception disappear. That is liberation in terms of perception.

His cognitive ability no longer remains bound to the light computer or neural computer in the brain. He additionally activates his quantum computer with infinite computational speed and thereby gains access to perfect intuitive knowledge. His knowledge base stays no longer limited to his treasure of experience, nor that of his ancestors or society. Instead, he gains the freedom to know anything he wants to know by tapping into the universe's database at the finest level of space.

He becomes a cosmic individual whose perception and cognition are infinitely extended, not even limited by space, and who is therefore in harmony with all the systems of his body, especially also with the subtle nervous system in his heart."

There he communicates with the Omniscient and the Almighty through his personal Avatar, who is available to him 24 hours a day.

"Since his perception is no longer limited, he feels noble feelings towards all beings in the universe. Wherever he looks with his infinite perception, he sees nothing but his Self.

Using the same method of Siddhis, he even overcomes the bondage to planet Earth by changing the gravitational field through yogic levitation.

Therein lies the genius of Patanjali, to enable the yogi, by binding attention to one place, to attain liberation."

So there is really no limit to what we can achieve. In conjunction with our personal Avatar, our individuality can recognize and achieve anything in the universe. In the next chapter, I will take a closer look at how far this goes.

15. The Power of the Almighty

In order to describe the power of the Almighty, I would like to summarize what we have viewed so far. The word for this from our opening verse is 'sahitaṁ'. It means a togetherness, a being connected with each other. Who is connected with each other? First of all, it is the two who have been mentioned before. 'Bhavaṁ bhavānīsahitaṁ' means that 'bhavaṁ' and 'bhavānī' are connected. Shiva and Shakti enjoy their oneness. Pure knowledge and its organizing power are intimately connected with each other.

How great is pure knowledge? It encompasses everything. Therefore we call Ishvara the all-knowing. His knowledge side is Shiva. His power side is Shakti. How great is her power? She too encompasses everything. Therefore, we call Ishvara the Almighty. When she expresses her power, Ishvara appears as Shakti. We shall now examine the greatness of this power in more detail.

How great is the power of the Omniscient and the Omnipotent? Very great, one might say, for they are, after all, capable of creating and sustaining a universe. But that is not all. From quantum physics we have a more precise indication of the magnitude of their power.

If we consider the smallest structures in space, then we know an exact value for it, namely the Planck length. This is the smallest distance which still makes sense. In chapter 2 (The universal computer) I described it in more detail. It is 1.6×10^{-35} meters.

If one now calculates all possible oscillations which can occur down to this order of magnitude and adds them all up, one comes to the so-called vacuum energy. This is the unmanifest energy of virtual oscillations, which exists everywhere in empty space.

It is not infinite, but nevertheless extraordinarily large. If we add up the total mass and energy of our 4-dimensional manifest universe, we arrive at 10^{55} grams (a 1 with 55 zeros to the left of the decimal point). If, on the other hand, we add up the unmanifest vacuum energy in one

15. The Power of the Almighty

cubic centimeter of space at any point in our universe, we arrive at 10^{93} grams. This place can even be in our heart. This means that the vacuum energy in each cm³ of empty space is enough to create our entire universe 10^{38} times. That is how great the power of the Almighty is!

Creating a new universe or dissolving one is no big deal for the Almighty. In the same way, it is easy for her to create a thousand or a million or a billion new universes. Even a separate universe for every human being on Earth would be easy for her. The energy for this is contained in the vacuum oscillations of the universe computer.

The universe computer is the information level of the knowledge of the Omniscient. On this level he has the power of vacuum energy at his disposal. So he knows everything and she can do everything. Through the knowledge of the Omniscient, the power of the Omnipotent becomes effective. Information alone would only be fragments. In order for them to be used purposefully and to achieve a powerful effect, the information fragments must be united into a whole.

That is the function of knowledge. It is the connections between the information that make the knowledge. That is also 'sahitaṁ'. The connection between the information leads to knowledge. It is through this connection that the power of the Almighty becomes strong. Shakti has an orientation. She aligns herself with Shiva, with pure knowledge, and thus she becomes strong.

Through our personal Avatar we have contact with the most powerful friend we could wish for. It is no problem for her to create a new universe. How much less of a problem is it for her to change just a few little things in our existing universe?

There are only such small changes that we want in one of the hundreds of billions of galaxies in our universe, in our home galaxy, the Milky Way. And in it also only changes in one out of a hundred billion solar systems and there also only on one planet a small matter rearrangement, like for example getting a new house built. Oh, how cute is that?

So when we ask our almighty friend to grant our cute little wishes, we don't have to worry about her ever running out of energy to do so.

Here another meaning of our word 'sahitam' comes out. If I have invited Shiva and Shakti to reside as Avatar in my heart, I am naturally connected with both of them. This is also expressed by the word 'sahitam'. There is a close relationship between me and my Avatar. Thus I can participate in the knowledge of the Omniscient (Shiva) and in the power of the Almighty (Shakti).

Solving the entire energy problem of the Earth's population is no big deal for the Almighty. There is enough energy for everyone! Dear children, you really do not need to fight over how to get enough sand on an expansive seashore to make your own sand castles!

To start wars for energy, water or other raw materials is completely insane. It comes from brains riddled with malware. We should no longer entrust them with the leadership of mankind. The best ruler, Ishvara can definitely do better!

As soon as people are no longer misguided by the limitations in their consciousness, an unimagined golden time is awaiting us on Earth, in which everything will be possible. There is enough energy for everyone. We only have to access it. The knowledge for this is shown to us by our personal Avatar. He gives us all the knowledge that we can just grasp and he filters the almost unlimited energy so that we can still cope well with it.

We can achieve as much as we can imagine. We can create a Heaven on Earth. More about this in the next chapter.

16. Divine Magic

What will Heaven on Earth look like? Through what will it come about? What will change? What will cease? What will come into being anew? How will we get there?

We get there through the last word of our opening verse. It is 'namāmi'. It means 'I bow down'. It means to lower the head and bring it closer to the heart. When we bow, we give greater space to feeling than to thinking. It is not an outward bowing, where someone throws himself in the dust before his statue of God or his image of God. No! It's not bowing to our smartphone either. No!

It is an inner bowing. With bowing, I embrace even more closely my Avatar, who dwells in my heart. With bowing, the bond with my Avatar grows.

I would like to dedicate this last chapter to Heaven on Earth. If people cultivate their connection with Ishvara, who dwells in their hearts as a personal Avatar, humanity can rise to a higher level of development. Thus begins the evolution to unimagined splendour at all levels of human life. A golden age is upon us.

Through our personal Avatar we have access to all knowledge. With it we can solve all problems. Problems exist only as long as their solutions are not known. With the knowledge of how they can be practically solved, the problems are already removed.

With the ending of problems, we can then unleash our full creativity. There are no limits to this, for the Omniscient to whom we have access is also the Almighty. They are not an external entity that we have to make a deal with. They reside within us.

So we are not given the divine magic from outside, but we transform ourselves so that we embody the divine magic. Our work is then not limited to personal matters, but affects the entire planet, our solar system and the universe as a whole.

One thing that will be set right in our solar system is the violation of Saturn. In Vedic Astrology Saturn is described as the servant. He is by his very nature helpful and not dominant. That too is described by the word 'namāmi', bowing down. So actually, everything would be fine if Saturn had not been hurt.

Vedic scriptures tell us that long ago the planet Saturn was unjustly treated and deliberately injured. The scars of this injury are still visible in his ring system. Hence Saturn has changed his character from a loving old grandfather to a disappointed bitter old man. Thus Saturn has taken on a leadership role that he cannot fill well, because leadership does not correspond to his true nature. He leads humanity rather clumsily through a series of external control systems that he has installed on Earth.

These control systems are controlled by the influence of the planet Uranus. Uranus was also hit in the cosmic accident of Saturn and changed its axis of rotation. It is the only planet in the solar system that does not rotate along its orbit around the Sun. It is transverse, so to speak.

Uranus rules all electronic systems. This is how Saturn's control is enforced on Earth, namely with electronic, artificially intelligent control systems. These include the Internet, mobile telephony and artificial intelligence, which controls these systems worldwide.

Saturn and Uranus obstruct the natural expansion of Jupiter. Jupiter expands knowledge, success and wealth. Unfortunately, it has been hindered for thousands of years due to the Saturn violation and the obstructed Uranus. As a result, Jupiter even affects Mercury very close to the Sun, causing Mercury to negatively affect all types of communication whenever it is retrograde.

The violation of Saturn symbolizes the fault of the intellect. It affects Mercury through Uranus and Jupiter. Mercury rules the intellect. With the healing of the Saturn injury, the fault of the intellect finally disappears. This fault is that the intellect thinks it is the real Self. Saturn thinks

16. Divine Magic

he is the Sun and he has to control people so they don't do bad things. But in doing so, he has not noticed that he has brought about an enslavement of humanity under these systems of control and unnecessary suffering.

Saturn is under a delusion, for the leading role in the solar system belongs to the Sun, and not to Saturn. The control of the world should not happen through the misguided intellect, but through the intuition that our Avatar gives us again and again.

Ishvara can heal the injury of Saturn if we ask him to. That is exactly what has happened now.

What will be the effect? All systems of external control guided by Saturn will disappear and be replaced by lovely, life-enhancing systems.

When the fault of the intellect disappears, so will all the intellectual control systems that the violated Saturn has installed on Earth through the intellectual thinking promoted by Mercury. These include:

- The Babylonian Money Magic with its relentless interest system
- The unjust judicial system with all its corruption
- Power and money hungry politicians without knowledge and experience
- A money-driven media industry that hypnotizes the great masses
- The pharma-driven health care system, which exploits people through ever new diseases
- A poisoned agriculture and environment
- A subterranean network of control by which alien intelligences have long controlled our Earth
- The fact-based, limiting and punishing school system
- The system of wars to steal resources
- Weather manipulation as a weapon
- Hidden biological warfare

- The inhuman, so-called new world order
- The system of karma with reward and punishment

Healed Saturn will once again become benevolent and serve our Earth and humanity with his gentle, quiet influence and with that, the unjust control systems will all disappear.

All these unnatural systems of control will collapse under the weight of their own mistakes. Thus the system of karma will fulfil its last great function. The bad karma of the control systems and their creators will destroy them themselves and thus abolish the entire karma system. Ishvara has the power to erase karma!

Then begins the renewed ascent of humanity. Infinite energy is available to us and we will create new things with divine magic. We no longer need to fight for resources. We will then become co-creators, using Ishvara's infinite knowledge and power every day anew and playfully.

We are in for a glorious time. There will be no more diseases. People will live as long as they want. We will be able to overcome gravity with our bodies and fly. We will live in inspired communities. There will be cities with high technological development and at the same time close connection to nature.

We will restore nature. We will end the depletion of nature and our Mother Earth will reward us. The deserts will be greened and there will be the right amounts of rain, wind and sunshine again.

Humans will become space travellers. We will be accepted into the cosmic alliances of spacefaring civilizations as the youngest member. We will explore space and discover new life forms and live peacefully with them.

Earth will become a jewel in the vastness of the universe. It will become a shining example of how fast a small planet can evolve. The Laws of Nature, the Devas will incarnate here. You will be curious to witness

16. Divine Magic

directly what changes of cosmic magnitude are taking place here on this small, third planet of the Sun Sol.

This is only a small glimpse into the bright future that lies ahead of us. If you also want to consciously experience and shape this cosmic spectacle, be part of it! Open yourself to the infinite wisdom and inexhaustible happiness that slumbers within you and is waiting to be found and lived by you. Find your personal Avatar!

There will be an advanced special course to unfold the divine magic. The course 'Divine Magic' will open up what can be additionally developed building on the Siddhi Power Training. With this we will make our contribution to the creation of a new, better world. We will enjoy this new world extraordinarily and make it more and more beautiful and magnificent.

Dare to take the first step and implement the recommendations in this little booklet for yourself as well as to please your loved ones.

www.ingramcontent.com/pod-product-compliance
Lightning Source LLC
Chambersburg PA
CBHW050449010526
44118CB00013B/1743